THE **EVOLVING** IMAGE

Ferguson

To Olive, the mother who kept my childhood drawings.

∾

To Isabel:

"The heart of her husband doth safely trust in her,…"

Proverbs 31:11

Solar Flare (detail)
In memory of Isabel Ferguson
Weston Public Library

THE **EVOLVING** IMAGE

Joseph Ferguson

Some of the text is from essays previously published in
the *Christian Science Monitor*:

"The Sculptor Seeks The Center Point"   October 1, 1985

"The Struggle Against Symmetry"   June 16, 1985

"The Artist's Eye On Creativity"   January 30, 1986

"The Artist's Education"   April 8, 1987

"Elizabeth"   February 24, 1989

The Evolving Image

by Joseph Ferguson

Revised August 22, 2011

Credits

Rod Nordell, Editor, The *Christian Science Monitor*, who first published
my writing.

David Van Vliet, a friend who, without a whip, hastened me on.

Jacqueline Dembar Greene, who provided gracious encouragement with
the craft of writing.

Photography

Cover photos by Andy Caulfield

Andy Caulfield, pages ii, 1, 8–9, 10, 13, 14, 17, 19, 22, 24, 26, 27, 30, 31, 34, 37, 38, 39,
    41, 42, 54, 58–59, 61, 62, 64, 66, 68, 69, 72, 74, 75, 77, 79, 80–81, 86, 87, 88–89,
    92, 93, 95, 97

Damianos Photography, pages 32, 33

Corey Davis, the Yellow Submarine, pages 55, 56

Isabel Ferguson, pages 2, 23, 60

Joseph Ferguson, pages 3, 4, 6, 7, 15, 18, 28, 29, 36, 43, 44, 45, 46, 47, 48, 49, 50, 51,
    52, 53, 57, 63, 65, 67, 70, 71, 73, 76, 78, 84, 85, 90, 98

Edward Hopfman, page 61

Book Design & Production

Susan Trevithick & Matt Mayerchak

ISBN: 978-0-615-70542-2

Published by:
Joseph Ferguson
joe@4fergs.com
781-893-4273

Printed in USA

Contents

The Utility of Images: An Introduction

Image — likeness, a reproduction or imitation of the form of a person or thing, — a mental concept or picture of something not actually present to the eye, — a corporate image.

Webster

All our ideas can be reduced to images, and these images constitute our reality.

On Intelligence, Hippolyte A. Tain, 1828–1893

According to Sebastian Seung, the self is a non-material entity. The 21st-century soul, however, is not some strange ghost in the machine. It's information. You are, in effect, a piece of software running on the wetware in your skull.

Julian Baggini

In the best of all possible worlds, my choice of a career would have been engineering or science, safely within the practical world of social acceptability where jobs are found and success measured. But I had little of the logical disposition that these subjects seemed to require. My desire and talent was to make things and draw pictures, to express myself creatively. I did not find numerical symbols, language structure, and memorization to be congenial or compatible with my natural inclinations. I was eager to learn — but not to study. I had more interesting things to do than homework and only learned to study late in life.

Art came to me as the alternative, the only thing I felt I was good at. I believed it was my choice, but I was mistaken. But, while I could demonstrate skill in drawing, I was terribly ignorant of the power of art to possess its practitioner and to transform existence.

Art ignores the rules of logic; it revels in contradiction. Why are so many artists wildly popular for a time, and then forgotten? Why was Vincent Van Gogh not

recognized during his lifetime of lonely poverty? Now, the sale of a single one of his paintings would make him unimaginably wealthy. He would be courted by the art world and live among the rich and famous, where cutting off one's ear might be seen merely as a display of eccentricity or machismo, or at the worst, a minor embarrassment.

Art is a puzzle. Why can't we all just make pretty pictures? The answer, I learned, was that more is required of an artist than drawing and painting pictures. I was told that an underlying mental component is required to create imagery, to externalize art.

Imagery is essential to planning, advertising, business and entertainment, literature, and all the arts. Some would argue that images are the medium of our thought. Imagery is common, increasingly pervasive. Yet, are art and imagery synonymous?

I'd like to share my personal experience with making images, with being an artist — specifically, a sculptor. My criteria for image making include bringing something

Meter Made, 1965

Singularity in progress

into being, creating something dimensional, colorful, in space, to express the images in my mind in a form of reality that others can experience. A painter does this with color and the illusion of perspective on a flat canvas, but I prefer solid objects.

When I was an art student, it was necessary to pass a course in the history of art. For most young art students who believe that they themselves are making history, the study of art history sometimes feels like a tedious chore. For some reason, however, I found the subject fascinating and I did study it, and was surprised to learn that I did quite well in a final examination.

We were taught that the history of art began logically with pictures of the cave art in Altamira and Lascaux, France. The obvious lesson was said to be that cave art was man's first attempt at aesthetic expression, the beginning of Art.

My practical nature, however, was not content with this explanation. I've always regarded aestheticism as somewhat suspect, as the pseudo-knowledge of the idle rich, the aristocracy, not the common folks like myself. I felt there was something missing. Surely there was more to art than aesthetic sensibility, emotional reaction, or historical valuation.

It is often said that art *enriches* our lives, but more than enrichment, I see art as essential to our existence and the evolving human presence. Much more than expressions of emotions or sensibilities, art is our practical tool of transformation.

The cave people were living precariously at the edge of extinction, and all their energy must have been directed at survival. Would they have had any time or need to cultivate aestheticism? Perhaps the images on the cave walls were there to evoke some dawning religious or mystical sense. But in my young, inquiring mind — my theory of the beginnings of art — I favored and trusted the useful over the aesthetic benefit of art. I leaned toward explanations of art centering on the practical need to express ideas more than the emotional or intellectual hyperbole often wasted on the objects artists create.

In the following story of Orn, the first man to make an image, I've tried to imagine the conflict and promise of the beginning of art.

Right page: *Singularity*, 2011

Rose Window 1982, 6' wide
First Church of Christ, Scientist, Framingham, MA

Orn's Gift

Horse with Arrows, Cave Painting, Lascaux, France, ca. 15,000–10,000 B.C.

ORN HAD BEEN A GOOD HUNTER but now he was scarred and frightening to look upon. His legs would not move and he had to drag himself about the cave with his hands and arms. When the hunters left, he remained behind with the women and children who ignored him. He would never again leave the safety of the cave, never hunt as the other men did. They lived in a large, high chamber deep beneath the earth. Light penetrated dimly from the mouth of the cave. At night when the hunters returned, the women threw branches on the fire and it leaped high, throwing warm light and shadows against the limestone walls. The hunters dragged the heavy carcasses close to the fire. They all joined in butchering the kill with animated chatter. Some of the meat was devoured raw, while large joints were thrown into the hot embers of the fire. Burning meat and fur gave a fatty, mouth-watering savor to the smoke drifting through the cave.

Orn dragged himself near to the fire. There was water to drink in a depression in the cave floor, but he had not had food since the previous night's hunt when there had been little kill. The hunters had elbowed him away and fought among themselves. The women had little to eat. But this night's kill was great, and as the hunters butchered the carcass, one threw a meaty joint from the fire to Orn. He caught it mid-air with one hand and retreated into the shadows.

Orn knew that some unvoiced law had been broken — the hunters had fed him. They had once hunted together. Orn wondered why they had not left him to die outside the cave when they killed the cat that mauled him. He sank his teeth into the fresh meat and when he had stripped the bone of flesh, he cracked it with a stone and sucked the rich marrow inside.

After the feast, more branches were thrown on the fire for warmth and as a defense against animals entering the cave. The hunters, their women and children wrapped themselves in animal skins and slept.

Orn dragged himself into a niche far from the fire. His body craved activity. He closed his eyes to sink into the unconscious darkness that was his only escape from a meaningless life — but images of the hunt paraded in the light of his mind. His muscles tensed, seeing his former self, running, spear in hand, thrusting his weapon with all the weight of his body into his quarry. He had killed buffalo, deer, pigs and cats. But when his spear broke, the cat turned on him in an agony of claws and teeth that left him crippled. Now, retreating from the pain, his mind returned to the thrill of the chase, to the speed and craft of animals.

He recalled when, by weight of number, they brought a buffalo down and killed it with their small weapons. Orn had clung to the thick hairy mane of the beast's neck, slippery with wet saliva. He felt the moist heat of its breath against his cheek, could see terror in its eye so close to his. They carried the buffalo's carcass back to the cave to the wild greeting of the women and children. His fingers knew the skill of dissecting the carcass, careful not to dull

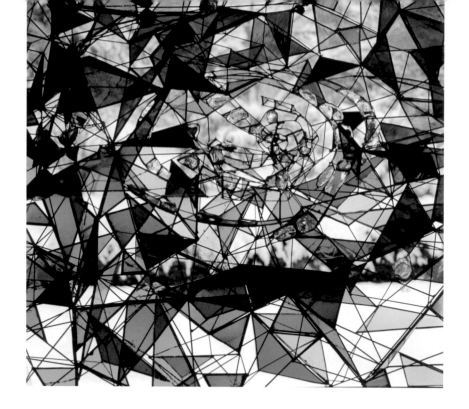

Expanding Universe, 1958 (detail)
Boston, MA, private collection

each careful stroke of the charcoal, his mind-image guided his hand. Quickly he outlined the beast's head, mouth opened, nostrils dark, but he knew something was missing. He paused uncertainly, then again he saw that large eye so terror-filled and close that it remained printed inside his head. His fingers sensed the contours of the buffalo's skull as if all flesh and hair were removed from it, to where the hollows of the eyes were. He placed the eye with confidence.

He paused again, regarding his work with a thrill of recognition. His mind teemed with images of all the other animals he knew. They were all waiting, in his mind.

Needles of pain made Orn wince, but the desire that possessed him was uncontrollable and stronger than any feeling he had ever known. He rolled his body along the wall, positioning himself to continue the line of the neck and the buffalo's heaving chest and forelegs. He changed position and staggered when the darkness outside the firelight seemed to flow into his head. Then he thrust himself out from the wall and continued the beast's mid and hind section, ending with the tail. His eyes closed as darkness relieved the pressure of the images in his mind; then he swayed and slumped heavily to the floor of the cave. Exhausted, he sat unmoving for some time, breathing heavily. Then he dragged himself backwards and leaned against the opposite wall of the cave. Turning his eyes up to his drawing, he gasped. His chest tightened and all that he heard was the beating of his heart. The overwhelming satisfaction that he felt could only be compared to the hunt itself and to the kill. His drawing had brought the images in his mind into existence; they could be seen, shared.

He wanted to shout, to make the cave echo with a peal of triumph but the hunters would not understand. They would curse him and sink back into sleep. He dragged himself past them, huddled in their warm furs, to the mouth of the cave. He pulled himself outside into the cold air. Faint stars waned in the pre-dawn light. He leaned against the cool grass on a bank at the mouth of the cave

the brittle blade of his stone knife against bone. The feast left him gorged, exhausted and gloriously satisfied.

No, he sighed deeply, these were only images in his mind. His legs would only support him painfully leaning against the wall. Yet, for a moment, the images in his mind were as real, as real as… He sighed again. What else was there for him to do than relive the life he had known as a hunter of animals, a predator in a world of predators?

He cursed the images in his mind that kept him awake while the hunters slept. Why, why — ? He should have been left to die. His restless eyes watched the firelight bathe the contours of the wall above him, then fixed with concentration. Often he had seen stone formations that had the shape of animals. But now he could trace the bulging flanks of a buffalo protruding from the wall above him. Painfully, silently, he struggled back to the fire, selected charred sticks and returned to his place. With his strong arms he dragged his body upward, standing propped against the wall. The pain was only beginning. One arm supported him. Tentatively he drew the charcoal stick against the rough limestone surface, leaving a dark line. He'd often marked the walls before, but with scribbles that had no meaning. Now he saw the buffalo's head, and with and watched the sun appear on the distant horizon. As its light touched him, he felt the first solitary glow of human exaltation.

The Reason for Orn

What expression of life remained to a crippled hunter who could not hunt, who was cave bound? Orn was a burden on the fragile subsistence of his society sheltered in a cave against larger, stronger predators. Only a dawning sense of compassion spared him. He should have been left to die. His discovery that mental images could be brought into being, drawn, recorded, shared, gave him a purpose for living, a place in the society he shared.

Certainly, this was the beginning of representation, the discovery of the power and magic of visual expression — art. Cave art unlocked the tools of abstraction. Picture tools take the place of real objects. Though we may never experience them directly, we see the pyramids of Egypt, Monadnock Mountain in New Hampshire, or the Himalayas that border India. Pictures prepare a child for the experience of life and the natural world. Thus through the abstraction that images provide we see distant objects and formations that surround us in space, or entities so minute that they are beyond the range of our sensations and can only be pictured through imagination.

Prophecy, 1957

Seven Stars, 1978

10   *Trojan,* 1973

The Tools of Transformation

IT'S THRILLING TO ANTICIPATE THE USE OF A TOOL, a chisel or knife honed sharp on a stone. Skill and imagination are put to the test to use tools well. We can shape objects, iron implements with fire, hammer and anvil. Sheets of iron and aluminum can be fabricated with welding into ships and aircraft that carry us to far places on Earth. There is great satisfaction in planning to build and make things — but I think there is as much satisfaction in the physical work of pounding nails and sawing wood to see the framework of a house rise from its foundation. Creative, physical work has an immediate reward. My failure in public education led me to prefer tools of the hand to those of the mind. Only gradually did I gain the confidence to cultivate my mental tools. Perhaps this is what led me to see images as tools, like hand tools.

Imagery is essential to the pictographs of written language, to all the symbolic representation of the arts and sciences. Men and women dream dreams and see visions. Like Orn, they draw pictures, with the result that bridges are built, skyscrapers rise from the ground, human flight becomes commonplace. Imagery is both the mind's tools and it is the medium of dreams and imagination.

But unlike the hammer and chisel which can be set aside, tools of the mind are ever restless within us. Provocative, they supply both initiative and energy, demanding to achieve some realization. As with Orn when he could not use his energy to hunt, imagery supplied him with tools of thought to accomplish what could

only be thought of as magic. Tools of mind are relentless as thoughts dispel rest, as plans intrude upon our sleep, and as mindless entertainment — that we supposed was a just reward for work — reverberates noisily in thought long after it is welcome. Each one of our senses — touch, sound, sight, smell — excites images in our waking and dreaming consciousness. Distant landscapes, emotions, rhythms, fragrance, knowledge and experience mingle in the forefront of our consciousness, interacting in a transforming chemistry to become something unforeseen. We create the ever-changing experience called reality.

Images are seductive. Like the smile of a child, they distract and catch us for a reason. Not only do they inform, but to the delight of the advertising industry, images give form to thought; they suggest what to think, which action to be taken, what car to buy, how to dress, which political candidate to vote for.

The caveman's invention of picture making prompted a spectacular leap in human evolution. To us now, with our hindsight, it seems so simple to draw a picture. A child can do it. But from the beginning of life on earth there had been no man-made images.

Think of the immense leap made by shaggy beings, clad in animal skins and living in caves, to the pyramids of Egypt, the literature and political theory of Greece, the architecture and engineering of Rome. Another leap accomplished the soaring cathedrals, mosaics, stained glass and illuminated manuscripts of Medieval times.

Now we stand at the threshold of discoveries and exploration through particle physics and genetics. Man's first step on the Moon was the symbolic beginning of space exploration. Orn's discovery that pictures could represent direct experience, bring predatory animals into the cave, and that they were harmless, was miraculous. Where will such a dramatic leap from our present time carry us?

Images existed in abundance to my generation early in the 20th century. I merely copied them and they evolved in the environment of my experience and disposition to find expression. Now, with television and digital technology, computer generated imagery and instant communication, the possibilities for human transformation are accelerating. What do we wish to be, and where will the enhancement of our genetic code take us?

Instead of using images to achieve the settled life that I had envisioned for myself, my study of art in Edinburgh, Scotland, changed me — *art used me.* Every sketch, drawing, or design I made, every stained glass construction or sculpture, advanced me further along the narrow, divergent path away from the familiar one I knew. I would have liked to have known where I was going. Perhaps we all would like to know the answer to that question. I've been forced to make my peace with the unknown because at the beginning of many projects, no model or plan existed. There was no Yellow Submarine, nothing to copy; the objects produced had no previous existence or iteration.

Each project was attended by the energy of inspiration. But gradually, with complexity and detail, the realization came that hidden in the euphoria of inspiration were problems with no apparent solution. If I found no solution, my project would remain lifeless, a failure. Art is a demanding master, and the artist — him- or herself — is the only judge of success or failure. Solving problems is a constant, lonely struggle, but it is the means of creativity.

Perhaps the first caveman to make an image on the wall had earlier conceived a clear and satisfactory plan to his life as a hunter when his plan was cruelly interrupted. His vision of self dissolved into physical inaction with the breaking of his spear, the retaliation of his prey. He was forced to discover a new kind of tool — one that could not be held but was just as effective when wielded in his mind.

More than a predator like other animals, the crippled hunter opened man's vision to a wider horizon of choice and creative transformation. We may never know what really led the first man to make the images that transported him across the wide chasm that exists between the animal and the human. We do know that his vault into the unknown transformed him into a being that had not existed on Earth before.

We are different from the caveman. We live longer, eat better, have leisure, control our environment and physical comfort, cultivate knowledge, and overcome the boundaries of time, distance and space. We are transforming ourselves.

But now that images in our world have become overwhelming, how do we distinguish between those that merely repeat the warm, familiar ambiance of popular culture, and those that build walls of stability against the threat of the unknown and the unfamiliar that change brings?

What distinguishes the plethora of disposable images that bombard us daily from the few precious images that are art?

I think that images that contribute to human transformation, that harmonize with the certainty of change, are those of art. They are characterized by invention in any subject that contributes to our humanity: science, literature, music, dance, art. These are the images of creation that place something on Earth or in the collective thought that did not exist before.

Venetian Balance, 1984

Artist in home workshop, 2012

Biographical Notes

Discovering Art

When I was a child, drawing was to me a plaything, a toy. It was fun to sketch likenesses of things, to enter a personal world described with the lines of a pencil, or erased. I copied Mickey Mouse, Popeye and Olive Oyl. My mother's name was Olive — she kept my childhood drawings.

The inspiration for much of what I drew came from the popular media, the funny papers and comic books, The Saturday Evening Post. Colored images were scarce and expensive then.

I was fascinated to discover that the parallel lines of railway tracks, drawn to converge, give the illusion of distance. Telephone poles diminishing in size beside the railway track contribute to this illusion of space on a flat surface. This discovery was magical and thrilling. The magic was later enhanced by learning about the science of perspective.

I thought I should like to be an engineer, a scientist, inventor, or a test pilot, but failing marks in the prerequisite subjects discouraged me. Public education was painful. It left me with the notion that my talent for art was of little importance and that art was not necessary in the adult world where jobs were found and money was made. School left me with the long-held, burdening belief that I could not learn academic subjects — that learning came only through personal experience or a talent that found no encouragement. I expected more of myself than was expected of me.

Mechanical Drawing came to my rescue. Through the back door of mechanical drafting, I infiltrated the coveted field of engineering. But I was not content, as I still wanted to do art. I took an entrance examination and was accepted for tuition-free night school study at Cooper Union in New York City.

Working as a draftsman for the New York Central Railroad during the day, I admired one of the older engineers in the drawing room. He was a graduate of Cooper Union School of Engineering. Though cantankerous and opinionated, he was a model of what I wanted to be: successful, articulate, self-confident, and he was an engineer. I was puzzled that he was not content. He raged against the retirement age of 65, and much of his energy and company time were dedicated to trying to reduce his retirement age by five years. I wrote a vow on a small piece of paper and carried it in my wallet for many years. My vow was to pursue art since it was my only talent, the only thing I really liked to do. I saw no retirement age. I would draw pictures and make things, not spend my life waiting for retirement. This vow was a singular moment of personal illumination.

Later, reading biographies of great artists, I had some misgivings about a career in art. I was a well-behaved church-going boy. The Bohemian lifestyle had no appeal. Sitting in a Parisian café, drinking absinth and discussing art with intellectual friends seemed to me a boring waste of time. I wanted a normal and wholesome life, stable

Cityscape, 1958

income, no debt, time for hobbies, entertainment and relaxation. Great artists as usually presented struck me as a tormented, unenviable lot. Furthermore, many were poor. Born during the Depression years in America, I was determined to distance myself from the humiliation and anxiety of poverty. My expectations for life were minimal, but I also had little to lose and was ready to take any opportunity that came along. The Depression years of my youth were a lesson that the tragic life was to be avoided, not cultivated. Still, I had little clue as to the thrill of learning and the variety of prizes that my life had to offer.

My role model at the time was my dad. I would work a 9 to 5 job in New York City, as he did. I could imagine myself returning by railroad to my suburban home in one of the communities that border the Hudson River. It was a Norman Rockwell fantasy—a pretty wife would meet me at the railroad station. The car would be warm against the chilly winter evening. We would drive to our three-bedroom home where children and mongrel dog would greet us. After a day of image-making in the city, I would spend my time pleasantly occupied with hobbies, mild entertainment, polishing the car, and the annual reward of two weeks' vacation.

This picture was predictable and satisfying, as the image of the hunt must have been to cavemen. The fine arts of literature, sculpture, painting, poetry and classical music were at some distant edge of my popular culture background.

An invitation, which could not be refused, to participate in the Korean War interrupted this dream and my study at Cooper Union. I served in the 417th Engineer Aviation Brigade designing and building airfields in Korea. The most significant events of my military experience were two visits to Japan where I saw Tokyo, Osaka, Nagoya and the temples and gardens of Kyoto. The harmony of architecture in its natural setting left a memorable impression.

On completion of two years' military service, I was rewarded with the opportunity to attend college supported by the GI Bill. I was eager to study abroad. The Edinburgh College of Art in Scotland accepted me for a four-year course in art on the basis of cartoons I had drawn while in the service.

The Edinburgh Experience

In September 1953, I sailed from New York City on the Cunard liner, Mauritania. Steam ship travel was less expensive than air in those days. Tourist class was made up almost entirely of students. The five days spent crossing the Atlantic were blissful. When I got tired of sitting in a deck chair enjoying the sunny blue sky and the ocean air, there were shuffleboard and deck tennis to work off the wonderful food. There were so many pretty girls around that it was hard to settle on one. In the evening there was housy-housy—a form of bingo—and dancing. After two years of military service, nine months of which was in Korea, I felt as if I had arrived in a heaven where romance could be cultivated. Nina emerged as a focus for this notion. She was American, returning from vacation in the States for her second year abroad at the University of Bristol. She had dark hair, child-like pretty features, and an air of worldly sophistication infinitely larger than her petite stature. When we docked in Southampton, at her invitation I joined her. We journeyed by train together to London where I spent my first night in England with Nina's sister and family. The following day we strolled on Hampstead Heath and our relationship began to look like the undying romance I'd dreamed about in high school and during military service. But that evening I entrained to Edinburgh, she to Bristol in the west.

Arriving in Edinburgh, I took a cab to the Art College. Senior students greeted me in the lobby. They had been assigned to help the freshman class find appropriate digs. We walked across a broad, grassy meadow opposite the college to a block of austere, granite apartment houses on Warrender Park

Terrace. I was introduced to Mrs. Lennox, first landlady on the list, and we took to one another instantly. She escorted me to my room on the third floor. It was spotlessly clean with a coal fireplace, a large wardrobe, bed and comfy chair. The window was open, and without central heating the September air was damp and cool. Gradually my room became a warm and comforting retreat, a place I was eager to return to each year after summer vacation. I remained with Mrs. Lennox for nearly four years. She was as generous and intelligent a woman as one is likely to meet in a lifetime. I had accommodations, meals, laundry and a coal fire at night. As the winter months advanced, a hot water bottle appeared in my bed. I wrapped my pajamas around it and placed them under the covers. When the fire in the grate turned to ash, I'd nip into warm pajamas, snuggle into a warmed bed and kick the hot water bottle down into the frigid depths to keep my feet warm.

Nina's letters came less frequently and finally she wrote to tell me that she had found an old love in Bristol. I was naïve to expect a brief shipboard romance to last. With four years of college ahead of me, Nina's painful but quick release was appropriate. The brief desolation I felt was soon replaced with the exciting life I found myself in.

Edinburgh is the capital of Scotland, a city of tradition built on the wealth of commerce and the quality of its institutions of education, medicine, engineering, theology and the arts. Like all the cities in Britain after the war, it had a tattered, smoke-grimed appearance. My arrival coincided with its rebirth — the Festival of Britain and the Edinburgh Festival.

The effects of war remained evident in scarcity, though Edinburgh had not been bombed. By contrast, in London there were gaps, like missing teeth, in street facades, and walls buttressed with timbers to prevent them from falling into weed-filled bomb craters. I acquired a ration book

so that my landlady could buy extra meat. Fuel was scarce, coal was delivered by open lorry, carried by the bagful up flights of stairs and used sparingly.

Landladies were reluctant to take American girl students because they required hot baths more than once a week — outlandish! Students wore dark clothing, warm wool sweaters and jackets and had an unwashed fragrance that I soon ceased to notice, having acquired it myself. Mrs. Lennox purposely fired up the boiler for my weekly bath. If I missed it, I would have to wait another week. Few students were so fortunate as I was. Landladies were notoriously stingy, slices of bread were counted. Mrs. Lennox's husband, Adam, rarely spoke a word but he was a supporting presence, as were the cat and dog.

Americans were scarce. As the only one at the Art College, I was a curiosity. To my new colleagues, Hollywood movies and the war alliance comprised my background. A precocious lass admonished me in her thick brogue, "Why day no have black Americans in your Congress?" Another, a husky version of Alan Ladd, the movie star, had been demobilized from a tough British paratrooper regiment and regarded me with some suspicion. He was not a man you'd want to cross. Military experience and age gave us a commonality but he shared the British serviceman's grievance against Americans. He told me of a movie he'd seen in which the Yanks, under the command of Errol Flynn, had driven the

Japanese out of Burma without any help from the British — the only troops that had actually been there.

I discovered that class dominated British society, though no one would admit to being among the lower classes. One point of admiration for America was that it appeared, at least in movies, to be a classless society. Here, the upper class, by inheritance, school tie, title and land, conveyed an invisible aura of privileged superiority that extended to Americans or anyone else, but attitudes were changing.

It would seem obvious that what I learned in four years at art college was of a social nature. I had time to think about living, how other people lived, and the life I wanted to create for myself. The mechanics of art were explored. I did life drawing and draped life drawing, design, study of color in painting, and craft work in pottery and glass. But I entered my course of study with the intention of being an artist, and I embraced all the experience around me.

Being an outsider has been the recurrent pattern in my life. During high school in the small dairy farm community in upstate New York where I grew up, I was the city boy to my classmates, though I worked the family farm as many of them did. In Edinburgh, I was the Yank, treated with fascination and suspicion. And since then as an artist, I have often felt foreign when people ask if art is my hobby. I suppose we all want to belong. More recently, since taking up golf, I honestly feel that I have at last made it in the field of social acceptability.

Running Tide (detail), private collection, Weston, Massachusetts, 2001

The Art College

It was a large, red sandstone building with a set-back from the road. Darling, the porter, held sway in a glassed-in booth center lobby. A tall, heavy-set man, he greeted everyone entering the lobby. I later learned that when there were questions, Darling had the answers. Messages were left with him. He was an animated communication device.

My class was in two sections of approximately 30 students each. The prettier girls inevitably were in the section I was not in. The students came from diverse parts of the Empire. I was the only one who did not speak English with an accent. One voice had an Irish lilt with a scattering of incomprehensible Celtic words, others the thick broad Scot's accent that came from islands in the far north where there were no trees. I could not understand them until aided with translation. I learned that ears were lugs, braw was good, and a pig could be a hot water bottle. English with a South African accent sounded American. Refined or upper class accents were evident and resembled the dreaded English invaders. Posh accents were acquired at the very best schools in Scotland and denoted superiority. Few students in my class with potent accents were protected by an invisible wall. As a curiosity, an American, I had a limited access to any class.

The curriculum was academic, including life drawing, draped life drawing from plaster casts of Roman and Greek sculpture and design. We began life drawing by buying a single large piece of paper at the arts materials shop. Paper was surprisingly expensive so the single sheet was used both front and back and made to last all day.

I learned a powerful lesson in life drawing. After studying my overlabored drawing of the model, the instructor drew a single line from head to foot over my wooly sketch. His line gave strength to my drawing by capturing the weight of the figure, as a plumb bob guides the stability of a structure.

Our life models were a curious lot. One tall, angular woman wore a black ribbon around her neck, in mourning for her deceased husband. A coal black Nigerian student from the University modeled occasionally. He had a wonderful, gleaming body and should have been a pleasure to draw, but he never held a pose and as time went by, he would end up completely turned in the opposite direction from where he had begun the pose. There was always a tranquil smile

Andrew Grant Bequest

Travelling Scholarship

Joseph Ferguson.   1957

DIARY from July 2nd – Sept 12th.

England

July 2   Fairford: St. Mary's church – interesting sculpture of the 12th.

3   Painswick;

4   Cirencester: Brasses – 14th. cent. armed man and his wife.

Wotton-under-Edge: Brass – 1392.

5   Bath and Swainswick: Brass of priest 14th. cent.

6   Wilton: Glass 13th. cent. taken from Paris, Sainte Chapelle.

Salisbury: Brass – Bishop Wyvil 1375.

7   Stoke D'Abernon: Brass – 1277 of a knight;   1327 of his son.

8   Studio of Mr. William Aikman, stained-glass designer.

10   Victoria and Albert Museum: 12th. – 15th. cent. glass.

11   Holland Park Sculpture Exhibition.

12   Canterbury: Glass of the 12th and 13th centuries.

France

July 17 – 24

Paris: Sainte Chapelle; Notre Dame; Museum of Modern Art;
Cluny Museum; Sacre Coeur; Chartres.

25   Sens Cathedral: 12th cent. windows, four, near floor level.

Auxerre Cathedral: Many 13th cent. windows at apse end.

Veselay: Church 1120. Formerly a monastery for pilgrims to see
relics of Mary Magdelene.

Charite: Founded by Cluny monks in the 11th cent.   Cathedral
now has modern glass, one window designed by Picasso.

les: Glass of 13th cent.

uroux.

gny: Church showed the transition from Romanesque to Gothic;
also beautiful capitals, carved, Romanesque.
Modern church – St. Pauls – windows thick glass, set in
concrete; two Romanesque churches:- Rodegrande and
Notre Dame La Grande; also Museum of Merovingian Art.

Diary continued.

1   Angers: Tapestries of 1375 – border very similar to that of Bishop

Wyvil brass in England, same period. Cathedral – modern glass

and 13th cent. glass in apse.

.1   Le Mans: 12th cent. glass in aisle, 13th clerestory.

2-4   Chartres: 12th, 13th cent. windows; also sculpture on West Door.

Luce (near Chartres) Modern church, glass set in concrete.

6   Rheims: 13th cent. glass.

7   Paris: Notre Dame.

St. Denis: Fragments of Abbe Suger's glass, 12th. 13th cent.

8   Avignon: Papal palace built in 14th cent.; Musee Lapidaire – sarco-

phagi; Musee Calvet; Pont du Gard.

9   Arles: Roman amphitheatre, theatre; Church of St. Triomphime 1

cent., Romanesque, also cloister; St. Trinquetaille,

10   Musee des Beaux Arts; Cathedral St. Sauveur, baptist

12   Aix: Matisse Chapel. Copper-wheel engraving by Hautin O

14   Vence: Villefranche: Quay-side Chapel, decorated by Jean Cocteau

Italy.

Aug. 15 Genoa

16   Florence: Uffizi; Cathedral; Baptistry St. John; Church

13th cent. glass; Medici Chapel; Acoademia Belle Arti;

National Museum; S. Miniato; Santa Maria Novella/

22   Siena: Pinacoteca;   Cathedral.

24   Perugia: National Gallery of Umbria; Civic Museum; S. Dominus, church;

University for Foreigners; Roman mosaics;

Assisi: Basilica S.Chiara;   Basilica S.Francesco; Cathedral S.Rufine.

Malatesta Temple; Church of St. Augustine.

Arti; Mosaic Group; Mausoleum of Theoderic;

Nuovo; Galla Placidia;

National Museum.

Ducal

of modern

ramic and

i – dramatist.

Diary continued – 3–.

Germany.

Sept. 5   Munich: Industrial Museum; Haus der Kunst – contemporary painting

and sculpture; Cathedral, 14th cent.glass, modern glass.

7   Augsberg: Cathedral – 1120 glass, bronze doors; St. Ulrich's Minister.

8   Ulm: Cathedral.

9   Strasbourg: Cathedral;   Museum l'Oeuvre de Notre Dame – 12th cent. glass

10 Frankfurt.

12 Brussels; Musee des Beaux Arts;   Cathedral.

Gemscatter (detail), 1983

on his face, his way of dealing with the monotony of a 20 minute pose. Another older man, an Italian, assumed his pose by tearing a large piece of paper or lashing out at an imaginary opponent, then holding the position. He said he had posed for great sculptors in his native country. Only occasionally we had a very pretty younger woman with a great thatch of curly red hair and pale pink skin. She had a childlike nature and mixed easily with the class during breaks.

Quite by chance, while studying in Edinburgh I met my future wife, Isabel Gomersall. She and her mother were in the parlor of my friend John's house and I came in one day after walking John's dog. His mother rented student accommodations, and they were there to talk to her about renting a room. Isabel was to begin the study of history at Edinburgh University.

We became acquainted and, over the following three years, we became engaged. We were married near her home in Surrey, England. Upon graduating, I was given a scholarship to travel through the art centers of Europe. It was called the Andrew Grant, after Andrew Carnegie, a Scot who had made his fortune in America and was famous for endowing many libraries in America, as well as academic institutions in his former home country. (See Appendix.)

Together we embarked upon a honeymoon that focused on the art and architecture of the cathedrals of England, France, Italy and Germany. Stained glass was the core of our study, but mosaics, tapestry, sculpture, painting, and all the flowering arts of Western civilization were all there. The tour was strenuous, but it provided a wonderful basis for a young married couple to develop and build a shared interest in the extent and beauty of art.

Our academic study of history and art became a total immersion reality. We began in the south of England where we visited Canterbury Cathedral. Then, crossing the Channel we moved on to the sights of Paris — Notre Dame, The Louvre and St. Chapelle — where the movement of light and the projected color of stained glass left a lasting impression that continues to influence my work. We rented a motorcycle and visited the cathedrals around Paris — Chartres, Bourges, Le Mans, Sens and Auxerre, and Potier — to the Riviera and the Matisse and Jean Cocteau Chapels. Then we traveled on by rail to the Medieval walled city of Carcasonne, to Avignon and the Roman Pont du Gare. By bus to Italy, the bronze doors of Ghiberti and the Michelangelo David in Florence, the mosaics and tomb of Galla Placidia in Ravenna and Rimini. Returning north to Belgium and Germany, and then back to England, we finally returned to the United States. We settled in Boston for a while before moving to suburban Weston, Massachusetts.

My four years' study in Scotland and my scholarship travel with Isabel had become the sure starting point for my career in art. Kodachrome slides supplied me with the visual material and the confidence to teach and lecture on Medieval and modern stained glass, and a solid background in the imagery of the European artistic tradition was now the springboard to my creative expression. All that I had seen provided the foundation for a lifetime of making art.

Why Stained Glass?

I might have been a painter whose colors literally flowed effortlessly onto the canvas or watercolor paper. I suppose there is some concentration but no visible sweat. And I've yet to hear of a painter being crushed or maimed by a falling painting. To set up an exhibition, he or she can transport the whole show in a small van. Even large paintings are light; they don't require scaffolding, riggers, a crane and a shop steward to put them on the wall. Paintings are easily rearranged.

I should have been a painter, but I am a stained glass artist and a sculptor.

There is no surface for stained glass color to flow onto. Like a picture puzzle, it must be constructed, each piece of colored glass cut to shape and fixed into a supporting matrix or armature. Sculpture has to be carved from hard materials such as wood or stone, cast in bronze or fabricated from welded aluminum or steel. Chiseling, welding and casting are hot and dirty, energetic, uncomfortable and fraught with threats to health and life. I imagine an ironic death: "Sculptor crushed beneath his statue dedicated to Life."

Sculptors don't cheat by creating the illusion of space as painters do. Painters don't have to represent what the backside of their subject looks like. They only give you one view. Sculptors are generous to excess; they present all the possible views of a subject. Think how many paintings that would be.

Sculpture doesn't sit passively nailed to the wall. It demands interaction, blocks your view, occupies real estate. If you're careless, it can do you harm.

Sculpture is heroic, but if I had had any sense I would have stuck to drawing pictures and coloring them — small ones — miniatures. Ignorance, youth and a fascination with the use of tools abetted my desire to build and create form in space. I wanted to expend energy, give patrons their money's worth in raw material and hard work.

In my choice of stained glass as a medium, I was fortunate to have another role model, William Haley. He worked as a stained glass designer for the Rambusch Ecclesiastical Arts Co. in New York City. When he heard that I was studying art, he invited me to tour the studio where he worked. In a high room sculptors were modeling a crucifix several stories high to be cast in metal. On another floor craftsmen were assembling mosaics. Mr. Haley led me into a darkened studio with a high skylight against which a stained glass window had been assembled. He showed me his design for the window.

I was struck that adults were paid a living wage for having so much fun. Now I feel embarrassed when I recall my admiration for William Haley. What a trial I must have been to the man as I contrived to sit near him on our return train ride home. I tried to engage him in conversation about the heavy art books I carried so conspicuously. His eyelids would droop and eventually I

Monhegan Island, 2005

realized that he merely wanted to doze off unmolested. I was content merely to be near him.

Later, when I was an art student, I often found myself working in the stained glass room. The teacher came in only occasionally and offered helpful suggestions. There were few other stained glass students. Chagall and Roualt were among the few modern artists that saw stained glass as a creative medium.

But I was reluctant to consider dedicating my life to a craft that I held to be somewhat suspect. The quotation from W.S. Gilbert, of Gilbert and Sullivan, "I'm not fond of uttering platitudes, in stained glass attitudes," summed up my feelings. The sentimental appeal of stained glass and its long tradition as a religious art had worn thin. What had I to do with stained glass?

Starbirth (detail), 30"square, 2001

Reflections on a Life's Work in Stained Glass

Symbolism and Experimentation

Orn's pictures of animals must have inspired awe. Pictures evoke intense emotional and intellectual response, confidence, fear, pleasure, awe. Mathematical equations may be explained as cathartic, wicked, beautiful, elegant in their simplicity.

Without symbolic representation we would be limited to the narrow world defined by physical observation. The arts and sciences depend upon symbols to teach and build upon past knowledge, to explore, communicate and record achievements. Artists create images to explore and give form to worlds beyond appearance and sensation. The mental pictures we have of God, Moses, the prophets, Jesus, and the familiar stories of Judeo-Christianity come not only from the literature of the Bible but also from evolving artistic expression of the times. National identity plays its part in the artist's rendering of the face of God and Jesus. They appear to be Latin. Widely circulated prints by Albrecht Durer lend the Deity Germanic, Anglo-Saxon features.

When I left art school in Scotland, I thought that I could bring a modern relevance to medieval symbolism of European stained glass. The extended period of rebuilding bombed cities after World War II provided opportunity for the artist. The Modern Movement required a reappraisal of all the arts. Medievalism and Art Nouveau were on the wane. In college I had been experimenting with new methods of fabricating colored glass. I wanted to say something appropriate to the times.

In *Prophecy* (page 7), experimented with the notion of revitalizing the old symbols but gradually came to rely on the effect of light, color and structure alone. Whatever meaning these elements convey is not precise as mere picture symbols and this fact avoids the pitfalls of sentiment and fashion. Reliance on color and structure of stained glass alone allowed for freedom of personal interpretation.

Modernism and Experimentation

As an art student I was indoctrinated. "Why draw and paint to achieve dimension and realism when a camera does it effortlessly, more realistically?" Technology hence gave birth to the doctrine of Modernism. Modernism rejected the sentimental pictures and imagery of the past, the Gothic and the seductive romanticism of Art Nouveau and Classical Revival, the images I had grown up with, the pictures I had copied. Artists who employed skillful realism — Norman Rockwell and Andrew Wyeth, for example — were derided as mere illustrators. Picasso, Braque, Salvador Dali, Matisse, and countless others were the popular stars of Modernism, the guru artists of my student days.

It was the same in all the arts. Architecture was dominated by Modernist theory and became undecorated, machine-like. Design was dictated by the notion that "form follows function." The Bauhaus left Europe and invaded the free world to dictate architectural style that influenced the rebuilding of cities after World War II. The tendency was for large buildings to look like glass milk cartons. In America, Frank Lloyd Wright championed harmony with nature and left the private house, Falling Water, in Mill Run, Pennsylvania, as a supreme monument to his personal interpretation of Modernism. Le Corbusier encouraged the plasticity of poured concrete. Architecture became sculptural in Eero Saarinen's TWA terminal at Kennedy Airport. Glass walls opened public and private buildings to light, reflecting the success of public education and a literate society's need for light.

As a young student, I could see that the medium of stained glass was stalled in a distant time. A vibrant, light-animated color medium cried to be rescued from centuries of flat, leaded technique, obsolete symbolism and gloomy architecture. Fifty years earlier, at the beginning of my century, Matisse and Pablo Picasso exhibited paintings that broke so many formally accepted rules that they caused a storm of controversy. Their paintings were dismissed

26

Solar Flare, 2010 (both pages), Weston Public Library

Moonscape, 1958

as ugly or unfinished, but they were the beginning of a new way of looking at reality — a way that profoundly influenced the time in which I was to live and work. There was no creative reason to draw pictures of the natural world around me. I was free to use the natural beauty of light- animated colored glass set in a structure of any material I chose to find creative expression.

Modernism encouraged the creation of new forms in all the arts. This inventive aspect appealed to me as had the inventions of scientists and engineers. Modernism was evident in the vibrant, unmixed color of Miro, the multiple forms of Cubism, the surrealistic imagery of Dali and the English sculpture of Henry Moore.

In dance, Martha Graham abandoned the stylized, graceful movement of classical ballet for the natural, angular movement of modern day industrial society, accompanied by distinctively modern music. Serge Diaghilev commissioned the Russian composer Igor Stravinsky to compose music for the dance, "Le Sacre du Printemps." Audiences rioted and critics called it ugly, but gradually modern dance and music have become accepted and have enlarged the possibilities of expression in these arts.

Poetry, design — all the arts — joined the Modern Movement as if it were a new religion. I saw evidence of the change in the work of my fellow students at Cooper Union in New York City and in the Art College in Edinburgh, Scotland. I visited exhibitions of the new modern art at the Tate Gallery in London, where controversy arose when one of the directors refused to exhibit Henry Moore's work. Now Moore is well represented by the Tate.

Modernism was distinct, a readily identifiable movement. I found inspiration in British modernist sculpture, in the work of Jacob Epstein, Henry Moore, Barbara Hepworth and Lyn Chadwick, and the metal sculpture and mobiles by the American, Alexander Calder. Though I didn't realize it at the time, I had become a Modernist.

I was fortunate that few modern artists beyond Roualt and Chagall had found expression in stained glass. I was entering a field with few players.

I experimented in various ways to fabricate stained glass in three-dimensional sculptural form. Since building boats and birdhouses in my grandfather's basement, structure had always fascinated me. Now I sought how to build, how to contain glass, how to make a sculpture that would survive in the landscape. Stained glass is a wonderful medium, but it has a problem. The dim architectural setting of a cathedral is as essential to its performance as is the dark theater to the projection of colored images on a screen. Unlike paintings and most colored surfaces, the rich colors of stained glass bleach out with surface illumination. The greater intensity of light must be behind the glass, rather than on its surface.

This problem had to be taken into consideration in any sculpture intended to exist in the landscape. Since there was little modern stained glass at the time, I had the opportunity to experiment in every piece of commissioned or free work I undertook. The soldering iron was my first tool to fabricate glass constructions, but soldered joints have limited strength and thus limited the size of projects. Welding offered a solution to the structural problem and allowed me to build larger pieces.

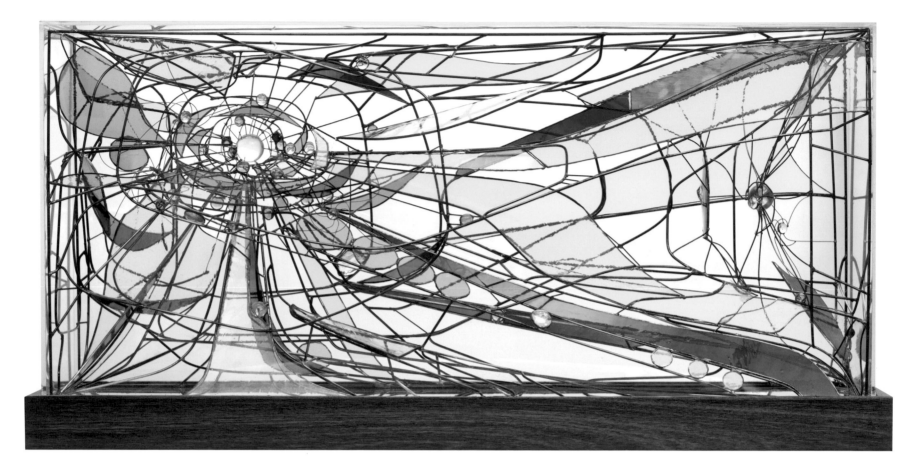

Lemondrop, 2008

Stained Glass Screen Constructions

Glass can be set in almost any medium: wood, concrete, plaster, stone, plastic, metal, etc. In ancient times, colored glass was set in incised alabaster windows.

I wanted to make three-dimensional constructions that suspend colored glass so as to appear to be free-floating. Screen Construction was the most successful means of doing this. The name, though clumsy, has stuck for lack of a better one.

The fabrication technique was suggested by the Tiffany lampshade in which small pieces of glass are bound with a thin copper foil, laid against a form and soldered into place. Larger pieces of glass required heavier copper foil. I built a wooden frame to support an armature of brass rod which would, in turn, support the pieces of stained glass. Instead of soldering the pieces together in a flat plain, I separated and superimposed them within the depth of the wood frame to produce a design of subtle variations in color. The space between pieces allows light to come through and become part of the composition.

A wooden frame, round or square, is required to enclose the composition and to give depth and support. Brass rod inserted in the frame at various levels takes the place of the armature in medieval stained glass windows. The support and linear expression of the design begins with bending the brass

Elements, 2008

rod. Connecting various levels adds strength. Once the design becomes self-supporting, glass pieces can be cut and bound with foil to be soldered into the armature.

I work directly as a painter does to make changes by adding or subtracting. If necessary, the brass rod structure is easily modified. Cut and bound shapes of glass are easily unsoldered. Texture and glitter can be added by inserting jewels of thick fractured glass, or blown forms that give additional dimension to a work.

Screen constructions need clear glass protection from the elements but are much lighter than a leaded glass window. Natural light floods the interior to enhance the contrast between the intensity of clear and colored light. Screen constructions meet the architecture's requirement for a light interior and allow the artist to change the composition easily.

The Crystal Pyramid

Working on a small cube sculpture, I wondered what it would be like to be inside the cube or any glass structure, looking out. My mind is never far from the application of stained glass to sculpture in the landscape. I mentioned this to my son and he suggested the pyramid as a simple geometric form that would sit well in the landscape. In that moment I could almost see a glass pyramid as an architectural sculpture. It could be illuminated at night!

The pyramid has strong symbolic associations and returned me to my quest for an appropriate symbolism that would make the best use of stained glass in the present time. The ancient pyramids were built as tombs for the Egyptian aristocracy, monuments to the secret mysteries of an afterlife. They were intended to be impenetrable, dark and mysterious.

A colored glass pyramid is the ultimate contrast to darkness and mystery. It will manifest the light-animated transparency so essential to modern life — the enhancement of civilization, not death. It may be experienced by the public, who need no religious or aesthetic indoctrination. Their only need is a child's delight in colored glass.

I build a blue and a red scale model at 1 inch to the foot. The blue model has a 24-inch base and the red, a 30-inch base. A video of the models is being made to help secure a client and site for a full-scale Crystal Pyramid. The full-scale structure of the work would be a truss work support dictated by the design, rather than a predictable, geometric, engineered pattern as in the I.M. Pei pyramid at The Louvre, in Paris.

Crystal Pyramid, 2002

Macrolux, 1977

Elizabeth: Lessons from a Stained Glass Restoration

Stained glass has the prestige of both art and craft, and it can be a good business. Commissions for churches and public and private buildings, as well as teaching and lecturing, offer a source of expression and income. Repair and restoration also provide income and recognition. It was through my conversation with Elizabeth that I came to value some of the lessons that art has to offer.

A friend told me of a window of historical importance that was to be installed in the newly built Newton Wellesley Hospital library. It needed restoration. We found it in a dark basement, thick with dust and in a heavy wooden frame, fastened to a four-by-eight plywood panel. With effort we managed to get it onto the roof of my station wagon. Restoration is not my favorite activity.

When I set it up against the afternoon light of my studio window, Elizabeth came to life standing amid her field of lilies. I had no idea that I would be entertaining a young girl in my studio. Our acquaintance was so sudden that I neglected to greet her. She said nothing and I wondered, "What is she thinking?" Her face is no artist's invention but a life portrait common to memorial windows. It's a child's face — but? She has been staring out of her window for nearly a century. Born to a wealthy Massachusetts family near the turn of the 20th century, she died at the age of four.

Accustomed to working in my studio alone, I was surprised to feel the presence of another person. My eyes kept returning to her and I noticed with concern that age and neglect had brought her near the point of physical collapse. I began to feel good about rescuing her. Gradually, perhaps out of courtesy, I fell into conversation with her. I said that her high-button shoes reminded me of yellowing photos in my grandmother's album. She observed that the works in progress around my studio have no pictures.

I explained that as a young art student, I had once been inside St. Chapelle in Paris on a stormy day. There, the outside noonday sun touching the windows kindled them to a blaze of reds. Colors projected onto the stone floor seemed to set it afire and reflected upward, warming the interior of the intimate chapel. In a moment, swiftly passing clouds quenched the sun and the windows transformed through purple into smoldering blues. The air around me pulsed with rich color, like music, ascending and descending. Since then I have tried to recapture that animation of color and light in my work. I've been less interested in stained glass pictures.

Elizabeth's eyes and lips are vitreous enamel fused to the surface of the glass. Her life-like appearance is the result of skillful painting and craftsmanship. By way of compliment, I call attention to the beautiful lilies surrounding her that give strength to her figure.

Suddenly aware of her cold silence I pause, glancing up to meet her eyes. She doesn't say anything, but I can sense that she resents my dwelling on technique and craftsmanship, which have a tendency to depersonalize her. If we're to have a dialogue I must not talk down to her, as if she were a child. Before I can apologize, she challenges me: "You're hiding something from me."

Hiding? Why do I feel so defensive? Then I remembered the slide in my lecture on stained glass. I include it because it's so ugly. It illustrates how opalescent picture windows, in her style, clamor for attention. Instead of color harmony, they give their architectural setting a muddy light. I recall that I only agreed to restore Elizabeth on a whim. Guiltily I move away from her penetrating gaze.

The opalescent picture window took America by storm in the late 19th century. Such windows decorated churches, office buildings, restaurants, and fine houses of the day. They imitate the pictorial effect of paintings through the use of a milky-colored glass. Painted enamel colors, modeling and linear

Elizabeth, Hewton-Wellesley Hospital Library restoration, 1989

perspective contribute to the window's impression of space. As quickly as they came into vogue they went into decline and became old-fashioned. The better examples that have survived by Louis Tiffany, John Le Farge and other artists of the period are enjoying a revival now. Some are very fine examples of a brief historical period, but they are nothing like windows of the 12th and 13th centuries.

I study Elizabeth, appraising. Am I prejudiced?

The opalescent glass artist preferred large pieces of glass to paint on. Lead structure was kept to a minimum, tolerated only because it was essential to hold the window together. Elizabeth's figure illustrates this. The dark outline of the lead can be seen around her face, hair, and shoulders, painted on one piece of glass. Her midsection and the bottom of her skirt are two other pieces of glass.

Opalescent windows push the technical limitations of the medium to the breaking point. They haven't survived as well as cathedral windows done hundreds of years before them in the Middle Ages. Those that remain require special care and frequent restoration. Pressure from a strong wind against the brittle glass is absorbed by their soft lead matrix. The larger the piece of glass, the more vulnerable it is to breakage. Elizabeth's face and dress have survived remarkably well but the leads surrounding her figure need attention. I resolder them and reinforce the lead with a copper strip. With care, she has her chance at immortality.

There I go, exaggerating, talking to myself about technique and history, evading my uncertain feelings about Elizabeth. The studio has grown cool. I check the wood stove, feeling her eyes on me.

European cathedral windows of the 12th and 13th centuries represent the high point of stained glass art. Their pictures are subordinate to an abstract composition of jewel-like pieces of colored glass. Painting describes form, controls light, and adds contrast to intensify the rich color, as do the leads, designed to be the linear outline of the pictures. They maximize the contrast between dark structure and the light-animated glass.

Windows of this style don't shout for attention. They harmonize with their interior architectural setting to produce a heavenly light. It is this abstraction of color and light that people talk of when they mention the blue of Chartres Cathedral.

I pause uneasily with the feeling of one who has lost his audience. Then I glance up at her, sensing her determination to have the last word.

Elizabeth airily dismisses my passion for aesthetics. She pooh-poohs my concern with structure. She manages, as aristocrats do, without seeming to display bad manners, to say that I am prejudiced. She doesn't care for dark old church windows, craftsmanship or the limitations of my knowledge. She won't be ignored — she demands that I like her as she is.

Art tests as a child tests an inflated balloon with a pin. It provokes and surprises. Art sets up a vibration between object and viewer, like the tension in the dialogue between Elizabeth and me. Art can be in the warm emotional pictures and stories that windows like Elizabeth tell, as in those that combine a perfection of structure and color from past centuries.

Elizabeth speaks art's timeless eloquence and challenge. She refuses to be ignored.

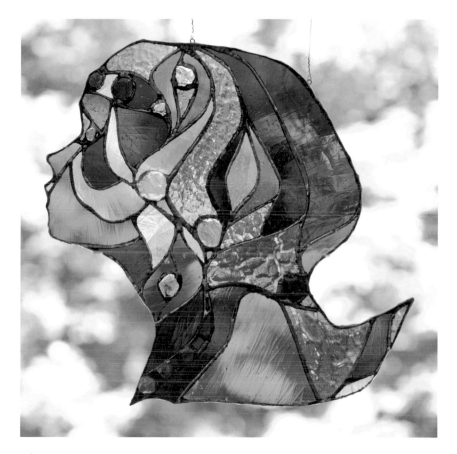

Sylvia, 2008

Carnival

Crucible

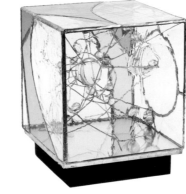

Bubbles

Two Essays

Style and Balanced Motion

That a moving form can achieve balance is immensely pleasing. That a sculpture, a dancer, or an athlete can maintain equilibrium echoes a pleasure in us as intimate as upwelling laughter, a sob, or the holding of one's breath to the end of a perfectly executed performance. The very nature of balance is that it requires precision, an exact center point. There is no "almost." Balance excites response; we feel its absence as a sense of unease. Something is wrong, out of plumb. It may topple over.

But the sculptor who uses this principle of balanced motion incurs a debt to Alexander Calder, the American sculptor who enlarged the meaning of the word "mobile" from adjective to noun. Calder's famous mobiles are an example of one man's exploration — in a sense, "discovery," of a new frontier in art — that of balanced motion. The close identification of Calder's name with the general principle of balanced motion provides us with an illustration of style.

Style is what distinguishes one from the many, and may eventually describe a branch of creative art. To the artist, success in his own eyes and in the eyes of history is achieved through a distinct style, his or her personal form of identity. It's difficult to surpass an innovator. There is great risk of being called merely an imitator. For this reason many young sculptors, in their search for artistic identity, avoid balanced sculpture.

Balanced motion is a general physical principle. It doesn't belong to Alexander Calder. But in the world of sensation and ideas, the names of artists identify territory and chart boundaries. Many ideas, sounds, procedures that on the surface seem open to common use are forbidden to one in quest of individual style. Territoriality exists even in the world of sensation and abstract ideas. Some of these areas are the well-known theories of Einstein, Newton, Pythagoras — grand, complex ideas conjured up by the name of a man. To stray into their territory by accident or intent risks comparison or the brand of imitation.

I was startled by an illustration of this recently. The host of our local classical music station commented disparagingly that the piece he was about to play, the "Warsaw Concerto" by Richard Addinsell, was in the style of the Russian composer Sergei Rachmaninoff. Perhaps the announcer didn't intend the scorn that his words implied. (In fact his program notes merely repeated a phrase from the Grove Dictionary of Music.)

From the jukeboxes of the early 1940s, the "Warsaw Concerto" spoke to soft adolescent sensibilities, though it had no words like the popular moon-in-June hits of that era. It was unusual to have classical music in the jukebox. Crashing chords conveyed a message through haunting, romantic melody. It was fantastically passionate music, three movements of a piano concerto compressed in a single disc. Its popularity spanned the age gap and remains with us now. At the time it served for some of us as a tantalizing middle ground to the dawning sophistication of classical music.

Besides the "Warsaw Concerto," which he composed for the film "Dangerous Moonlight," Mr. Addinsell, an English composer, wrote musical accompaniment for many other films. But his composition of the "Concerto" illustrates a precise conflict with style or its lack. Without doubt, Mr. Addinsell had trespassed on Sergei Rachmaninov's territory. In all probability he was simply in need of theme music for a film. He was not alone; much of film music is borrowed.

Personal style has two time frames. In the present it is the lifestyle, characterized by rapid change, the fad that passes. It is today's superstars. It is the popular culture of our children's times. That other aspect of style is our legacy of innovative achievement — discoveries that enlarge, describe and map our

human path. It is charted with the place names of men of genius and good fortune. It is the path of civilization.

Robert Frost's poem, "The Road Not Taken," strikes a common chord: resistance to imitation, relying on one's own feelings, one's own style. Style is the balance point between the self of imitation and the unique, emerging self. Where do we put the weight? Payment must be made for shining in another man's flame. If we can resist the applause that familiar imitation readily provokes, there is hope of achieving equilibrium.

Creativity, the Path of Transformation

Linear is the opposite of creative thought. In the linear mode, we perform the necessary sequential activities of life — dressing, brushing teeth, breakfast, and the drive to work that seem mechanical, automatic, thoughtless. Linearity allows us to visualize an orderly progression from beginning to conclusion of a task. It can be represented or quantified. One begins a journey. The logistics, means of locomotion, geography to be traveled, the time it will take, can be accessed before action is taken in a list, a plan, a map. Linearity is a straight line of thought that takes place within the confines of what is known. Creative thought cannot be represented as a straight line. It is more like a spherical implosion. It begins with a vague, shadowy awareness that something must be done. When or where to begin is uncertain, but a commitment must be made. The starting direction may prove wide of an ultimate goal but its success lies in eliminating one of many possible directions that might be pursued. Since the goal of creative thought cannot be visualized, is unknown, there is no way of representing it — no map, no path. Our only guide is the realm of feelings, intuition and imagination. An optimistic state of mind is essential. Knowledge is necessary, but not when it inspires doubt or discouragement, states of mind that retard creativity. The story of the mythical flight of Daedalus and Icarus is evidence that ancient man felt that he should fly. They, the wise people, said it couldn't be done. Many centuries passed before such feelings became fact. The knowledge of practical human flight has passed the century mark, but its realization is the first step in a felt

Primavera, 1985

journey that may carry man beyond the stars. When a creative goal, as in the case of human flight, is attained, it becomes useful knowledge, bricks and mortar to the necessities of both linear and creative thought.

Creativity is not a team sport. It is usually attended by isolation and a lack of social and financial support. As the life of Vincent van Gogh demonstrates, a unique vision requires more than the span of a single life before its product can be understood. Van Gogh's life appeared to be a failure. Extreme mood swings — depression, apathy, ecstasy –attend the creative process. And there is loneliness, for how can one share what is not understood and is rejected by the wise? Van Gogh's brother, Theo, helped financially, encouraged through letters, and had faith in his brother's work. Had he not kept his paintings, they might have been destroyed. Theo's faith in his brother was certainly a creative act. Creativity is practiced in a timeless realm; it resembles play and invites accusations of idleness, dreaminess, irrationality, madness — but out of creative intuitions comes knowledge.

In fairness, I must admit to bias. I don't want to be misleading. There really is no such division between the creative and linear as I have drawn. Our lives are lived somewhere between these extremes. Knowledge and creativity have distinct temperaments that serve us. Knowledge responds like an obedient dog while creativity must be coaxed like a cat. It may come when you call — or walk away.

Is the sudden popularity of the word "creative" just a whim, a desire for novelty? Or is its use an unconsciously precise response to the mechanical excess of linearity so profoundly felt that the risks of creativity become acceptable?

Machines that use memory and logic may account for some desire to shift toward creativity. Artificial intelligence gives us reasons to question past assumptions about human intelligence. The computer is programmed to mimic linear thought. Thus far, machines are not creative; they merely apply large memory to defined logic. Computers demonstrate that memory is not intelligence but merely a mechanical process. If a machine performs linear thought better than humans can, what is human intelligence?

The muscle-replacing machines of the Industrial Revolution were threatening when first introduced. They took away jobs. Men tried to resist the change they made, to destroy the machines, but once the genie had been released it could not be returned to the lamp. Now the machines' promised release from physical toil has been realized for many. Computer technology offers a similar promise to relieve men from mental drudgery. As computers continue to assume men's burden of repetitive sequential thought processes, they will give time and stimulate individual creativity.

Yet we often hear it said, "I'm really not very creative. I have no talent for poetry, music, science, business." Who can predict the consequences of a single life, the possibility in everyone to make whole areas of knowledge obsolete? Albert Einstein's mother was no celebrity but she was the unquestioned link to Einstein's existence. Often we find ourselves in the envious audience, applauding the stars of the solo performance. But both player and audience share the display of human excellence.

There is a tendency to limit intelligence to what is known and measurable, to ignore the potential of imagination. Questions phrased to known answers decline the challenge of the unexpected, the unknown that surrounds what little we do know. Can what we wish and dream and imagine certainly be as important, perhaps more important, than what we know?

Notes on Major Works

Sculptured Concrete Window, Harvard St. Entrance
Old Cambridge Baptist Church, 1962

The technique of casting deep shafts in a concrete wall to be illuminated by colored glass was inspired by the French architect Le Corbusier in the chapel at Ronchamps. The shafts present a broad surface for the play of projected, colored light. This amplifies changing angles of projected color as the sun rises, moves from east to west in the sky and diminishes with the onset of night.

Creation, **Side Vestibule**
Old Cambridge Baptist Church, 1962

The composition depicts the elements of creation, fire, water and the universe. It suggests the constant activity of creation through watery evolution and changing states of matter. Above the turmoil of appearance is the calm constancy of order and purpose, suggested by an endless circle.

Sculptured Concrete Window,
Old Cambridge Baptist Church, 1962

Creation, 1962

Tree of Life triptych, Chapel
Old Cambridge Baptist Church, 1962

My first commissioned work was the windows for the Old Cambridge Baptist Church Chapel. Dr. Samuel Miller served as Dean of the Harvard School of Divinity and had been minister of the Old Cambridge Baptist Church. He and his wife, Molly, lost both of their sons in World War II. The window is a memorial in their honor.

Dean Miller was deeply interested in modern art forms of Christian imagery, and courageous to trust a young artist with little experience. He accepted my water-color design and I began work. I was thrilled to have a scholarly, receptive patron.

The three lancet theme is a tree of life with the alpha and omega as two key elements. (See Revelation 1:8 "I am Alpha and Omega, the beginning and the ending, saith the Lord, which is, and which was, and which is to come, the Almighty.")

The concrete form of the omega is the tree, growing out of the masonry that surrounds the windows. At its roots, thorns symbolize conflict. In the mid-section of the three lancets there are symbols of a fountain, the cross and fire to suggest nurturing purification and transformation. The top panels employ symbols of God: the alpha is central and takes the shape of compasses to suggest the ability to measure the universe. On the right, the dominant alpha is flanked by the sun as a symbol of life, and the seven stars for the days of creation appear on the left.

Tree of Life triptych, 1962

Child of Promise, 1962

A visit to the London studio of the late Hungarian artist, Ervin Bossanyi, inspired the "Child of Promise," a leaded glass panel in the style of the 12th and 13th centuries.

The mother is at the center of the composition. Encircled by the family, she portrays the qualities of the feminine: compassion, the mystery of love and beauty, the object of desire and creative fulfillment. The father in the background reaches up, drawing distant objects in the universe through his fingers. The child with arms upraised to the mother symbolizes the nurturing of a fragile potential of creation. The Child of Promise stands apart from the warmth of the family, his destiny in the creative unknown.

Child of Promise, 1962

Pierce Chapel, The Cranwell School

Lenox, Mass., 1965–1967
Architect: Peter McLaughlin

The design of the stained glass was the result of a close and early collaboration with the architect.

This commission came as a rare opportunity to be a painter in light, color and structure on a grand scale. The architect suggested a treatment of the windows similar to the Bertoia screen at the MIT Chapel in Cambridge, Mass. In that piece, the screen dropped down from a round skylight over the altar. Various-sized pieces of metal attached to rods that extended from floor to ceiling caught the light, creating an ascending pattern of lighted substance. Our vision was a filigree of color and light to contrast to the massive, dark-enfolded concrete structure of the chapel.

My visits to the Matisse chapel in St. Paul de Vence, the Cocteau chapel in Frèjus, and the Le Corbusier chapel in Ronchamps, France, had prepared me for this commission. I wanted to compose the linear and color composition on the spot, in the chapel, as a painter would. Each element of color and structure was to remain adjustable, until the whole was complete.

There are 26 windows in the elliptical circumference wall of the chapel. The window openings tilt inward in long trapezoidal forms, eight feet at base, tapering twenty feet high to a two-foot top. The window openings are two feet deep. A full-scale model of one window opening was built in my studio. It was adjustable to the changing angle of each window opening. Within this guide, twenty-six armatures were welded together of steel bar stock of varying thickness. Fifty three-quarter-inch angle-iron frames of varying size were fabricated to be hung in each armature. Glass was cut to fit these

I designed the spire of the chapel at the request of the architect. It was built from a model by a specialist in spire fabrication. Its installation, by helicopter, was televised and broadcast on The Huntley-Brinkley Report.

Pierce Chapel, 1965–67

49

frames. Extra alternate colors of glass were cut to allow changes. The bottom frames were large enough to accommodate near full-size sheets of hand-blown glass. I've always been reluctant to cut the beautiful hand-blown glass pieces.

In September, 1966, the armatures were hoisted into the window openings and welded to steel pins sunk in the concrete at the side. Clear plate glass had been installed outside the window. When all the armatures were in place, I wired the fifty angle-iron frames into each armature to create an exciting linear pattern. The linear pattern of each window was adjusted to harmonize with the other windows and then welded into position. With the linear structure in place, the precut colored glass was inserted into its appropriate frame. It was then possible to adjust the entire color composition of the chapel windows using the additional pieces of glass that had been cut. The glass was fixed permanently with clips and caulking.

Color was used symbolically. Four hot red windows, two on either side of the vestibule at the entrance of the chapel, portray the colors of blood, fire, war, and symbolize the world of emotion, the distraction and struggle of life. Passing through a screen into the main body of the chapel, there is an abrupt shift to a pervasive, enveloping blue light. It is meant to approximate the color of the west wall of Chartres Cathedral in France, the color of contemplation. Its blue contrasts to the hot reds, left behind in the vestibule with coats and galoshes. Shafts of clear white light pour through the open work of rich color to add a dynamic sparkle to what might otherwise have been a dark interior.

Pierce Chapel (detail)

The Christian Science Pavilion,
The New York World's Fair, 1965–1967
Architect: E. Durrell Stone
Interior design: Hadley Exhibits

In the opening year of the fair, a white obelisk soared 25 feet up into the star-shaped skylight at the center of the pavilion. It was a central feature of the Christian Science exhibition. The obelisk had slightly concave surfaces on which texts from Mary Baker Eddy's writings were displayed. I was asked to design and fabricate some form of stained glass adornment to add color, texture and emphasis to the obelisk. I built screen constructions of glass and metal and fixed them to its sides.

At the conclusion of the first year, the pavilion was closed to the public. I was invited to consider minor revisions to update the display for the final year of the fair. A committee met at the pavilion and Durrell Stone, the architect and designer of the pavilion, was also invited. He was the last to arrive and when he saw the obelisk at the center of his creation, he was not delighted. His scathing observation, "It looks like a marble grave monument" resonated under the high skylight. A memorial to death was not the committee's intent. They were in unanimous agreement when the great architect commanded that the offending cemetery piece must be removed. What was to take its place?

Stained Glass Tree 1, Christian Science Pavillion, 1965–67

Since my first screen construction designs were merely adornments to the existing centerpiece, I was grateful for the opportunity to design something to fill the yawning void where the obelisk had been. I made a scale model of a stained glass tree to be built of steel and glass. It was to be 14 feet in diameter and 28 feet high.

The size of this structure was daunting, far beyond the scope of soft soldering I was accustomed to using. I needed a stronger technique if I was to build a self-supporting tree. The medieval windows of the 12th and 13th centuries suggested a solution. Welding was the modern tool of choice to build steel structure. I had to become a welder.

As usual, I began with a deceptive, nonsensical strategy. I cut a 14 foot square hole in the floor of my studio. I live and work in a barn. The hole in the floor allowed me to work in the basement and construct 18 feet of the tree. The remaining eight feet would be fabricated separately. I welded a framework of steel bar stock into a tree-like form with arms that extended out seven feet from center. When this was completely prefabricated, soldered sections of glass bound with copper were constructed, suitable to be attached to the iron armature. When all the sections of glass were complete, I removed them and cut the armature in sections for shipment to the pavilion. I then rebuilt the tree and hung the glass sections to become a complete composition. Sections of the tree were sold after the fair closed and may still exist.

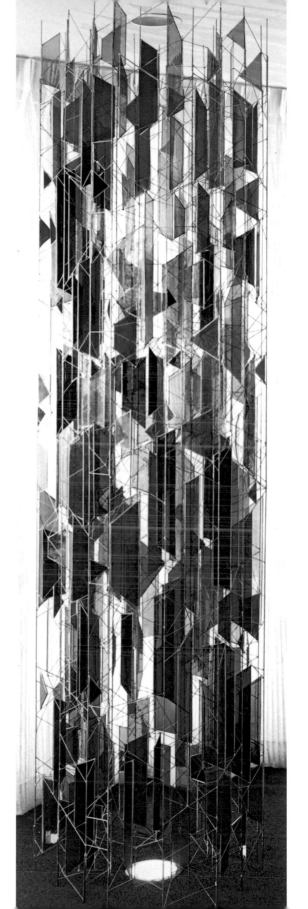

Stained Glass Tree 2, Christian Science Pavillion, 1965–67

Yellow Submarine, 1969

To climb up into its faceted globe is to embark on a voyage in time. Children warp into the future to see themselves as heroes in the grown-up world of adventure. Adults, more preoccupied with the moment, experience a reverse thrust, back to their childhood moments of timeless play.

When not on exhibition, the Yellow Submarine appears as a sculpture parked on my front lawn. Its conception began when I was an art student experimenting to find a means of removing stained glass from its architectural setting. I wanted to infuse landscape sculpture with the light-animated colors of stained glass. The name has little to do with its conception. A vehicular name was required, and the popular Beatles' film provided it. I had an

indistinct vision of a sphere and wings, supported on three legs (the minimum necessary for stability). One leg would provide step pads to allow children, or adults, to climb aboard, interact – become a part of the sculpture. The sphere suggests a large helmet, a diving bell or control-pod. There would have to be a seat under it so the pilot's head and shoulders could fit into the sphere. He or she would be bathed in color, see the world through facets of stained glass. I had a clear glass decanter top the size of a baseball that would serve as a handle for the gear shift lever and as a crystal ball for navigation.

The two commissions, the Christian Science Pavilion "Tree" at the New York World's Fair, and the windows in the Pierce Chapel in Lenox, Massachusetts, encouraged me in the belief that I was a competent welder. I began work with some iron bar stock of varying thickness left over from commissioned work. I like to start a project with materials I've already worked with.

I made some rough sketches to capture what was in my mind but I did not want a complete drawing or model. The spherical form and wings had to be designed with flanges to hold the pieces of colored glass, and porthole-like shrouds to shade the colored glass from direct sunlight. Wing-like forms would

arch over and around the sphere to form a glass ceiling. As the sun moved across the sky, the angles of projected color beneath would move, bathing surfaces below in rich, ever-changing color.

At first the work was thrilling and progressed rapidly, but with growing size and complexity, chaos threatened. Hard work took the place of play. With my oxyacetylene torch I cut away a previous week's work in a moment of doubt. Since there was no pattern to follow, I had to rely on feelings that the visual relationships were right or wrong. But feelings are often imprecise and can be mistaken. Tools that work fast and effortlessly lead to rash acts. Forced to visualize a replacement, I spent another week fabricating what I had cut away. Completion of the sculpture began to seem like a distant notion and receded into the unknown as I advanced more cautiously. Fabricating a large project in a direct, unplanned way is rarely attempted. It requires a naïve, energetic disposition, lots of time and a maniacal tolerance for self-induced frustration.

I began to wish that I had made a model. Ideas can be explored less painfully this way, and mistakes are easily corrected. What a fool I was! Why had I been reluctant to plan or make a model of my sculpture?

As I've said before, my first desire in life was to be an engineer, but here I was, an artist deliberately thwarting the elementary planning procedure that engineers, manufacturers and architects follow with such success. I gained a new respect for the beaver, a lowly rodent that has the sense to build a dam to make a pond so that he can raise his family in an underwater house. The beaver is a master planner.

My reason or excuse was that I wanted to create something that had not existed before, to bring a sculpture into being that I felt more than visualized. How does an inventor or an artist make something when he has no plan? Knowledge is a starting point, but I knew that I had to resist the predictable, lazy man's way, to minimize the influence of what I could fully visualize at the

start. I needed something more than what I knew. I needed inspiration that could only come from a dialogue between the sculpture and me. But it was hard, frustrating work and it took many months.

Spontaneity is fun, but it requires a timeless childlike disposition and it may lead to chaos, discouragement, and failure. Planning discourages flights of fancy and is tedious, but it forestalls costly mistakes. The Yellow Submarine effectively trimmed the sails of my spontaneity and taught me to value planning in the making of a large sculpture. But what seemed to be a failure of process proved to be a success in realization. The sculpture is whimsical in appearance, colorful and changing in the landscape and something I could not have anticipated. It transports voyagers of all ages to other states of mind.

Could I have planned it?

Yellow Submarine, 1969

Chromacopter, 2006–7

Stainless steel, glass and acrylic

Chromacopter is the realization of a long-held desire to improve upon the *Yellow Submarine*, 1969. I made several models to this intention and began work on the full-scale piece in 2005.

For practical reasons, stainless steel tube was used throughout the structure. I chose this material because it is lighter than the solid steel rod used on the Yellow Submarine. It has a long-lasting polish to reflect projected color, it glistens in the light and requires no painting or maintenance.

When this piece was completed, I cut it into sections to be joined by mated bolting plates so that the sculpture could be disassembled into 6 pieces for shipment. Flanges to contain the colored acrylic panels were welded on to the outside of the round tube. The acrylic colored panels were cut to size and caulked in place with silicone seal.

Much of the color media used was the recently developed dichroic laminated acrylic sheets. This material displays a rich blue or magenta color, a gold mirror surface, or near- transparency, depending upon the viewer's orientation. It is ideal to exploit natural light to change the appearance of sculpture in the landscape.

Children may enter the control module by ladder, under adult supervision. There are two seats to accommodate child chromatravelers.

Learning from my frustration in building the *Yellow Submarine*, I made several models of Chromacopter before beginning work. The full dimensions of Chromacopter, 24' long, 12' high, required lots of climbing ladders, much bending and cutting, many welded joints and hundreds of little hex-head stainless bolts. But I followed my model and there were few surprises. Certainly it could never have come about without the *Yellow Submarine*.

Chromacopter, 2007

Artist with *Chromacopter,* in progress

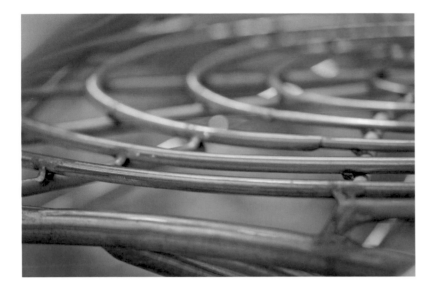

Chromacopter (detail), 2006–7

Sunrise on the Ocean of Time

Orn opened something more to men and women than the animal existence of time and space, pleasure and pain, birth and death, the risks of predation.

The circle is our image of time-less eternity, no beginning and no end. A timeless energy that is larger than our sun warms us, as it did Orn, with the life of the mind. Our destiny is to make images, images beyond our present capacity to imagine.

Sunrise on the Ocean of Time, at Weston Public Library, 1987

63

Pneuma (mobile), 1962

Viking (mobile), 1961

Chroma, 1994, aluminum and acrylic

Seraph, 1995

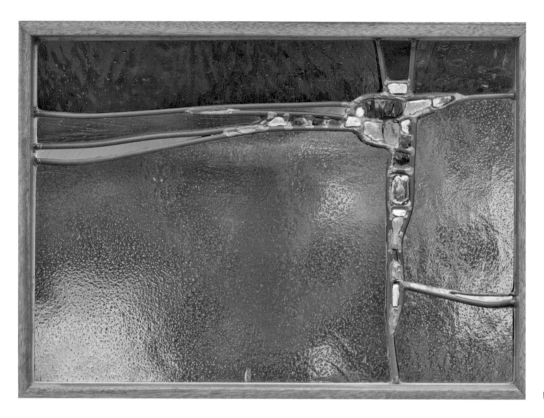

Where Two Meet, 2005

Green Harvest, 2005

Artist in studio, 2012

Other Media

Environmental Sculpture: A Fascination with Architecture

The commission work I had done was profitable and it gave me confidence and tools to build large sculpture. It also provided knowledge of materials with which to build the dimensional landscape sculptures I had envisioned as a student.

Sculpture and architecture have much in common. Often a building is referred to as sculptural, a sculpture as architectural. The utility of architecture sets it aside from sculpture. Though the environmental pieces were meant to be entered, they were purely aesthetic. They were to be experienced, not lived in. To enter the sculpture was to become a child again, to jettison the practical demands of adulthood for the joy of play. There is also something tranquil and meditative about stepping into stained-glass colors. Such sculpture must withstand wind, rain and snow. Unfortunately, the environmental pieces required the real estate and maintenance that architecture demands. The aesthetic delight they afford is prohibitively expensive. With regret I had to dismantle them or, as in the case of the piece commissioned for the Storm King Art Center in Mountainville, New York, it self-destructed in high winds, was rebuilt and succumbed to the same fate.

"Green Fragility" was sheathed in transparent glass and had a basket to contain growing things. A single seat afforded the solitary viewer space and ease to experience becoming a part of the sculpture. Viewed from outside, its faceted surfaces of glass reflected light, as mirrors dazzling in the landscape.

My inspiration for these sculptures was encouraged by the work of Antonio Gaudi of Barcelona, Spain, the Towers of Watts by Simone Rodilla, near Los Angeles, California, and the Palais Ideal by Ferdinand Cheval in Hauterives, France. This style of work comes under the fascinating classification of Futurist Architecture.

I regret that only pictures remain of my efforts to combine architecture and sculpture.

Green Fragility, 1973

Aluminum Form in Space

I had begun to question my reliance on the facile beauty of colored glass. Would my sculpture in the landscape be significant if there were no pretty colors, if I relied on form alone? I admired the sculpture of Henry Moore and Alexander Calder and thought to try my hand at large sculpture in the landscape. Building sculpture-in-the-round from flat sheet aluminum offered an exciting challenge. I began by making small, one-inch-to-the-foot models of soldered sheet copper.

Welding is both frightening and fascinating. The explosion of light, the sharp sputtering sound when an arc is struck, is pure pleasure. Developing skill and control over the concentrated energy to melt and weld metal is thrilling. Aluminum is a soft, durable, accommodating metal. Lighter than steel, aluminum permitted me to build large pieces to compete with natural forms in the landscape. Aluminum does not rust, it glows in the moonlight on the night landscape, dazzles in sunshine when polished. Beneath layers of protective oxidation, it takes on a soft, natural quality.

Model of *Animus*

Animus, 1988

The contrast between large, bold forms and small, intricate forms sets up a tension that contributes to a sense of movement. I scribed a grid on the model's surface and plotted corresponding curve sections onto a larger grid on the sheets of aluminum. Pieces were cut out and tack-welded together. When changes were necessary, the joints could easily be broken. When the full-scale sculpture was completely tack-welded together, I did a finished weld to all the joined edges.

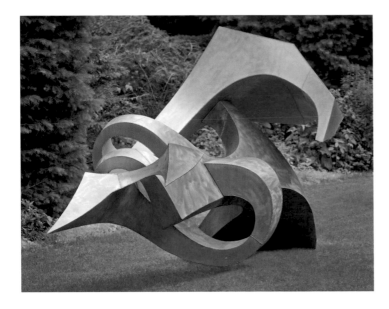

To compete with nature, sculpture must have size, monumental presence, contrast of material, dynamism, a surface that dazzles in the light. On coming closer, there remains much to be discovered by walking around, through, looking up at, and down upon the piece. There should be a sense of sharing, juxtaposing one's own spatial mass and rhythm with that of the sculpture. Children do this easily. In this sense, experiencing sculpture is akin to climbing a mountain, leaning against its upward thrust, resting in the hollows of cliffs or boulders, gazing out from its lofty elevation to a retreating landscape, descending into its valley.

Building large sculpture is hard work. Anyone who has built a large sailboat in the back yard knows the agonizing length to which initial inspiration is stretched. Getting inspired for a sculpture is like falling in love: it is exciting, but patience is demanded for the long term. Often the shape each sculpture takes is suggested by past work; this is called artistic development. Some works suggest an entirely new direction to pursue. Each piece makes its personal statement, though they all evidence a common origin.

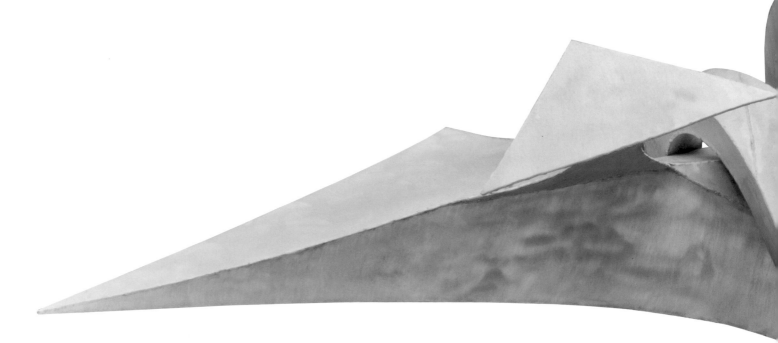

Narwhal, 1981

74

Starplough, 1981

Starplough, 1981

Surprise comes when predictable patterns are avoided. I've had a conch shell in my studio for many years. The outer shell has been ground away to reveal its inner spiral structure. Its influence on the aluminum sculpture, "Narwhal," is obvious. All forms—natural, man-made, stone, shell, tree, machine,—excite the imagination. Visual stimulation, imagination, and the drive to create sustain one through the hard work and mental frustration of bringing sculpture into existence. I've tried to be inventive, resisting the familiar themes that appeal to novelty, sentiment, sexuality, and violence,—the sure formulas to recognition and financial success.

Poised Energy, 1982 ; Brunswick, Maine Public Library

Zeus, 1980 (with *Starplough* and *Counterpoint* in background)

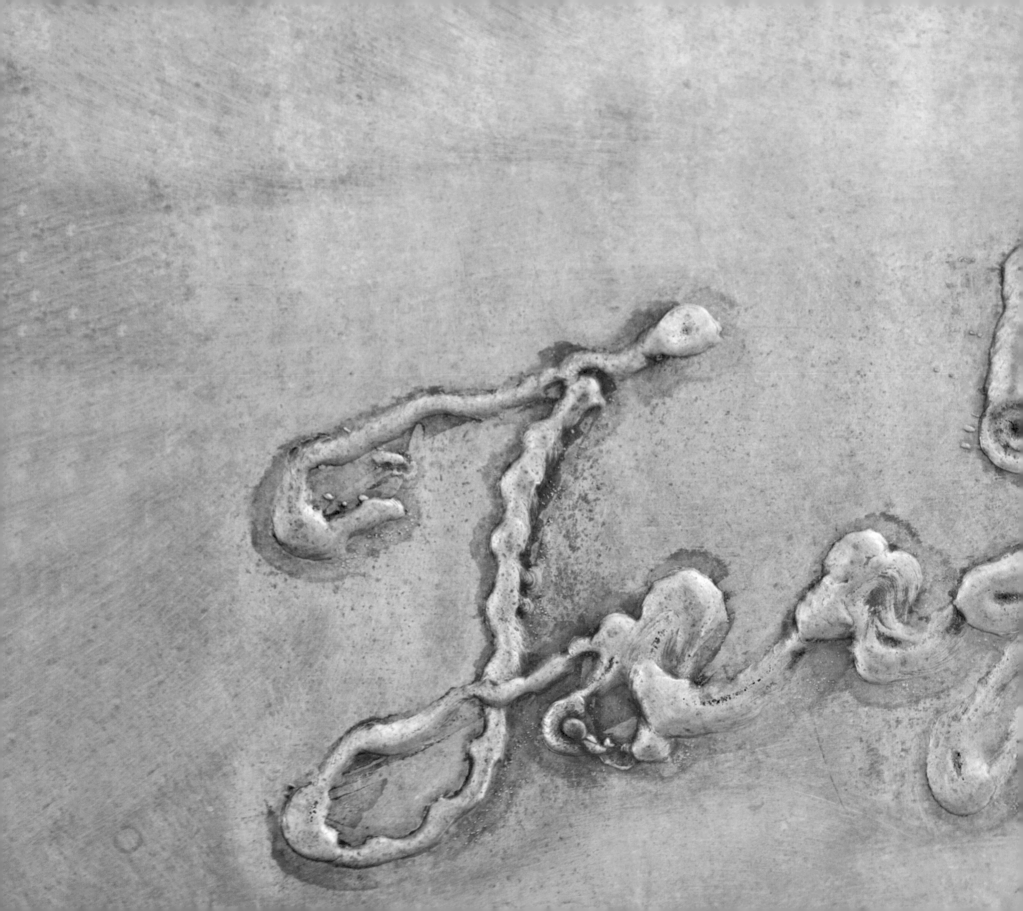

Essays on the Evolving Image

Where the Forms Come From

"What does it mean? What is it about? It looks like a bird — like, like a–?" Often people have trouble framing their question. It's natural to want art to look like something familiar, something we know and can respond to. But some art is outside our knowledge and experience. I've had visitors who tactfully pretended not to see the large objects intruding on their vision in the peaceful suburban setting of my lawn. They say nothing. Education that expands our mental horizon can narrow it to the sight of our eyes. There is a danger in seeing only what is known. Why are artists so perverse; why don't they just repeat all the familiar things, the trees, flowers, moms and dads, children, the familiar things?

The form my work has taken began with my childhood drawings that were readily appreciated as likenesses of the comics. A fascination with tools and curiosity about how things work contributed to the aesthetic structure in my sculpture and stained glass. The years I spent abroad in Korea, in the military, and in Scotland studying art of the past were formative. I learned something about color in Scotland. There was also the technical experience I gained while working, briefly, for Joseph Reynolds Stained Glass Studio in Boston, and the challenge of my first commissioned works.

Having experienced the unending hard work of farm life, I embraced mechanization and all the instruments and benefits of science and technology that intellectuals seem to fear. I wanted to find a place in the industrial age that I had been born into. Though I didn't necessarily want to be an artist, I did want to build, to make things.

The satisfaction in making things can only be experienced; it cannot be explained or conveyed in any other way. And in every artist, every maker, there is the overhanging threat, "If I don't make it, it will not exist." There is immense

satisfaction to doing and making, and perhaps that is why the craftsmen who actually do the physical work are so modestly paid. Though never acknowledged, many men do work for love of expression. A master carpenter confided to me that, while on vacation in Florida, he found himself in a foundation ditch helping the men lay out footings. Even more than the satisfaction of physical effort is the intellectual satisfaction of bringing one's thoughts into realization, leaving a mark in the earth, providing a step up for others who may need something to stand upon to extend their reach.

There is a common mental process in all creative efforts that employs the elements of contrast — repetition, tone and intensity, large and small, dark and light, — perhaps because these and other properties reflect some common emotional understanding and response.

The composition of music relies on variations of frequency, the rapid and slow, the bright soprano opposed to the dark bass; on pitch, the loud and the soft; on repetition of note and theme.

In poetry and prose, words are crafted to paint pictures and suggest mental landscapes against which a range of contrasting emotional response is enacted, from the bright and cheerful to the somber.

In some people's minds, great art deals only with death and misery, perverse sexuality and violence — the gloomy, rather than the bright, things of life. From the brief experience of misery in my own life, I've learned to avoid it and I do not intentionally inflict or cultivate the dark side in others. I've tried to shape my work in a way that will be beautiful rather than ugly, constructive over damaging.

Duck, 1965, 9' high x 7' diameter (*Suarian* in background)

The Impulse to Art

There is a compulsion in us to identify and name, to see unity, to give order to apparently dissimilar things and aspects of the natural world, to give a form of reality to the ideas in our mind.

On an island off the coast of Maine, there is a small community of lobstermen. Gray shingled buildings perch above the granite shore. From the sheltered harbor and pier an unpaved road ascends steeply past the island inn to join other houses, a one-room schoolhouse, library, store and church. Paths branch out from the road to the outlying houses of summer people. When my wife and I arrive the summer houses are closed, the people gone. We feel the chill of winter in the ocean air. The few other visitors who disembark from the small ferry with us are quiet, dressed in subdued colors, layered against the damp chill of the twelve-mile ocean crossing. They may be birders. The island lies in the path of bird migration. At night we have heard the birds and see their dark shapes silhouetted against the full moon.

In the evening we attend the Sunday night hymn service in the church. Inside, the church is warm, lit by gas lamps along the side walls and by a chandelier of four kerosene lamps hung from the high ceiling. Hymns are chosen by the small congregation. I feel strange, knowing the words to them when I have not sung them in many years. "Let the lower lights be burning, send a beam across the waves, some poor fainting struggling seaman you may rescue, you may save."

The congregation is an instrument of song. The church grows warmer. A brief sermon follows. "We must take time for life and the beauty of the island." The itinerant minister, flushed with the passion of our song, must wonder, "Do words have a place after such singing?"

The service ended. An elderly woman holds a flashlight to guide us down the few wooden steps into the blindness of the cool night. Forms disappear silently into its blackness, others linger for a moment to murmur in awe. We look up. The sky is a dazzling wonder, overwhelming in its vastness. The Milky Way, a luminous, glowing trail, arched from one distant horizon to the other, each constellation etched with the engraved clarity of a star chart. Splendor attends such experience.

Rest and Reflection, 2001
Traditions of Wayland, Independent and Associated Living
Wayland, Massachusetts

Right page: *Golden Sunrise* (left), 2001; *Landscape* (right), 2001
Traditions of Wayland Independent and Associated Living, Wayland, Massachusetts

Aesthetic moments provoke wonder. Our fascination with knowledge must have been inspired by such natural confrontations. Compelled to observe, one cannot ignore what presses in all about us. Mariners from islands like this observed the relation and change of stars and planets, marked their disappearance and return — and named them. Feelings of awe inspired the practical knowledge we now call the science of celestial navigation. Though reduced to a science, its name evokes a sense of wonder.

So pleasant is the aesthetic moment wedded to the dawn of learning that men braved danger and withstood the tedious labor of observation and recording. So we have named each star, insect, flower, bird and species of marine and animal life, the elements of matter and the vitalizing forms of energy. Learning has become a human passion.

Feelings of awe, inspiration, imagination, love, compel us to breach the protective walls and security of what is known, to venture into the unknown. We are like a single candle in the surrounding darkness of the unknown.

Guardian, 1971

Images As Weapons

The caveman's invention of imagery gave us the crucial tools of the mind. With them, we break away from the pack, mitigate the bondage of instinct and violence, escape the mindless darkness of the cave.But tools can be used as weapons, images can be used to reinforce the very irrational animal instincts that enslave us and obscure the light of intelligence. The weapons we forge to defend ourselves have often been turned against us.

When we use the imaging tools of the mind creatively, compassionately, generously, we express science and art to enhance humanity. When images are used cunningly to exploit, threaten or dominate others, they may be as effective as teeth and claws, the weapons of the animal world which the caveman knew only too well. He gave us the key to the better world we live in now, but animal predation remains with us.

Sadly, the images of commerce are crafted with scientific expertise as weapons to excite specific instincts and desires. Children and adults are targeted for coercive imagery. Invasive advertising clamors with noise and violence to distract and deaden thought, to promise instant satisfaction over long-term goals. Satisfaction, happiness, and healing are promised in bottles at the corner drug store. Commercial images cultivate the instinctual animal in us at the expense of the thoughtful and the human.

The wealth of imagery is controlled by commerce. Unless the ethics of commerce is modified to benefit society, it may smother our precious humanity. We must learn to control images so that they cannot be used, as they are now, against us. Narrow personal interests must not be permitted to promote lifelong addiction to alcohol, tobacco, chemical substances, or to cultivate patterns of behavior, in vulnerable youth, that are inhuman and socially corrosive.

Threat, 1985

Samurion, 1978

EPILOGUE
Where Are the Images Taking Us?
What Are We Becoming?

WHAT WILL THE FUTURE ARTIST'S PICTURE OF MAN BE? will it be a representation of godlike men and women like the marble artifacts or Greece and Rome or Michelangelo's heroic Renaissance depiction of David? Or will it find an image source in the spiritual mysticism of ancient religious thought?

Men and women left the cave and the hunter-gatherer existence to found agricultural communities and cultivate the qualities of the human mind, planning, social structures, arts and science — civilization. Yet we continue to revert to violence, war, murder and cruelty, to behaviors more appropriate to the animal than the human. Perhaps we have only taken the first steps along the road to being human? We live with a growing awareness of this paradox.

But no matter how flawed we appear to be, change has taken place for the better. I see few people returning to the cave. Once learned, the images of hand and mind cannot be erased. For life without imagery is literally unimaginable. Imagery and human evolution are inseparably linked. The greater part of what occupies our thoughts would not exist without the symbols, diagrams, sketches, photographs, models and recorded patterns from the past. An ever-increasing number of people have the access, time and opportunity to use symbolic tools to fashion personal creative expression. Presently, we live lives that are beyond the wildest dreams of our ancestors.

Our cave ancestors' first visual expressions in art were of the world of predatory animals they knew. Since leaving the cave, modern man's experience is of an ever-expanding vision, ranging from minute particles and invisible forces to the vastness of unnumbered galaxies like our own. We see clearly that we are not like other expressions of life on Earth. As men, we have the power to change our environment and ourselves. We may be only at the beginning, rather than at the end, of a unique evolutionary path.

Technology has dramatically affected the work we do. Instead of guiding animals harnessed to the plough, we find ourselves harnessed to the Internet, driven by interaction with ephemeral symbols on a glowing screen. Imaging technology connects us with the world and an increasingly vast creative expression that would have remained hidden to our unaided senses.

We see the rapidly passing reflections of ourselves in popular media, entertainment, communication and the arts. Certainty of change undermines past notions of a static reality. Continents drift, oceans form, mountains rise and crumble, climate changes, civilizations are born and decline. We cannot avoid the physical implications of species change that Charles Darwin confirmed through observation. Our present appearance as men and women is the product of evolution documented in fossil evidence, a gradual biological transformation from minute life forms in an aquatic environment to the Homo sapiens that now stands before us, clothed and, we hope, in his right mind. Our present appearance is not the finished product but certainly a passing shadow on the evolutionary landscape.

Technology is so pervasive and crucial to our existence that it influences the choices we make and our very survival. Biologists unravel the genetic code of all life on Earth. Cloning animals has been accomplished. Cloning humans seems inevitable. We've never been satisfied with the human body. Perhaps we can build a better one. Cosmetic surgery accommodates the novelties of fashion.

A sound mind in a perfect body has been man's goal since ancient times. Can scientists combine the best body and mind to make a perfect human being?

Will the artist's picture be a composite of popular mall culture cultivated by the advertising industry, an Albert Einstein's brain in Schwarzenegger's body? A compassionate Mother Teresa in Marilyn Monroe's body? Our dissatisfaction with mortality makes change certain. The science of nanotechnology envisions self-replicating machines of molecular dimensions governed by artificial intelligence. Eventually such self-conscious human devices may move

Samurion, 1978

throughout the universe, exploring, gathering knowledge, living happy, productive lives as we do. Will devices created by man relegate us to the dustbin of obsolescence and become the next link in the chain of human evolution?

Inevitably, technologies of machine and mind will influence what we appear to be. And what of the unforeseen leaps of dramatic change that no artist can imagine, self-conscious entities that have no form to inspire depiction?

In this turmoil of accelerating change, it's not surprising that we all long to return to that twilight stage of childhood consciousness when the world seemed to move slowly, to stand still in a golden age when men and women moved, as a flock of children, under the loving care of a divine father. Are we, as human beings, unique in all the universe? Are we created and governed by a divine, benevolent ruler? Will we ever understand the spiritual power of inspiration and intelligence that animates the human, the impulse of our creative nature? All uniqueness is challenged. Matter and energy are interchangeable. Energy is the animating potential in everything our senses experience. And like the seasons, the birth and death of stars, the rise and decline of civilizations, our planet Earth, the species man and all knowledge, will eventually return to the impersonal potential of energy.

Change is the only certainty. Is anything fixed and eternal — changeless?

Prompted by this perennial question, men and women from various cultures and periods of time have experienced creative insights that are the foundation of the world's great religions. Mary Baker Eddy, a 19th century New England woman who wrote *Science and Health With Key to the Scriptures*, expressed her insight when she wrote, "Creation is ever appearing, and must ever continue to appear from the nature of its inexhaustible source." Creation, energy and intelligence seem to be the interwoven threads of existence, of life itself.

Chromacopter, 2007

Was it idle chance that prompted a man to draw pictures on a cave wall? Was it the compassion of his hunting comrades that allowed him to survive and be granted time to make images? Our questions address more than the death of one man, but the death of our home planet, Earth, as well. For we know that light we see comes from stars that have long ceased to exist. So our sun will swell into a fiery ball of self-consuming energy, turning all life on Earth to ash. Eventually our nurturing planet will return to the energy that formed it.

Are the tools of mind that Orn gave us inadequate to deal with this certain, ultimate change? Is the artist's final image one of fire and ash, nothingness? Will the miraculous transformation of art survive the total annihilation of Earth? With the tools of mathematics, Albert Einstein expressed in his formula $E=mc^2$ our understanding of the transformation of matter and energy. Can the human leave its matter base and survive in the creative potential of energy? Ray Kurzweil, in his book "The Age of Spiritual Machines," comments on this question. "By the year 2090, most conscious entities do not have a permanent physical presence." Strange, unpredictable things happen. The injured caveman Orn gave weak predatory animals the power of imaging tools, the arts of mathematics and all the transforming tools of the mind to create and cultivate the human.

Now the digital age of computers and the Internet guide us along a divergent road. No present artist can model or sketch images of where this road to define the human leads. Personally, I look for the compassionate, animating hand of inspired intention — the hand of creation, the hand of a prolific artist. Often I've felt myself with the energy of the moment, in a state of childlike anticipation between mental image and realization balanced between the nothingness of apathy and blind repetition, and the allness of Life.

We are all image makers, confronted with a blank canvas, the sculptural space we move in, the infinite patterns of thought and ideas we entertain. To

the artist in each one of us, the world is teeming with the challenge of experience, the incentive to understand, a compulsion to create. Beyond money or fame, the satisfaction of building, creating, and understanding is a palpable, cathartic, euphoric experience. The artist is at one with his creation as a mother is with a newborn child. And we all are enriched, treading darkness, like stars, beneath the rising of each splendid illumination.

The qualities of mind that underlie human experience are changeless, perfection, love, compassion, intelligence, and creativity. These are the tools we work with. The Mind's substance is seen in man's ever-changing vision of himself.

We are the evolving image.

Chromacopter (detail), 2007

Featured Artworks

Green Gem, 22.5" square, 2006